A Guide to Pueblo Pottery

A GUIDE to PUEBLO POTTERY

WESTERN NATIONAL PARKS ASSOCIATION
TUCSON, ARIZONA

Library of Congress Cataloging-in-Publications

Lamb, Susan
    A guide to Pueblo pottery / [written by Susan Lamb.]
      p. cm.
    ISBN 10:1-877856-62-2(pbk.)
    ISBN 13:978-1-877856-62-4
    Pueblo pottery. I. Title.
    E99.P9133   1996   96-34657
738' .089'974-dc20   CIP

The net proceeds from WNPA publications support educational
and research programs in your national parks. www.wnpa.org

Written by Susan Lamb

Photography: Jerry Jacka, cover, pages 11, 21, 23, 27, 35, 41,
43,45; John Barry, pages 13, 15, 17, 19, 25, 29, 31, 33, 37, 39.

Cover pot by Stephen Lucas, Hopi, courtesy of McGee's Beyond
Native Tradition Gallery, Holbrook, Arizona

Design by Simpson & Convent

Printed in China

With thanks to Dick Howard of Santa Fe, New Mexico, for
sharing his knowledge and experience in the preparation and
review of this guide.

Quotations from potters courtesy of Stephen Trimble, from interviews con-
ducted for *Talking With the Clay: The art of Pueblo Pottery* and *The People: Indians
of the American Southwest* (published by the School of American Research Press,
Santa Fe, New Mexico; copyright © by Stephen Trimble, 1987 and 1993,
respectively).

CONTENTS

INTRODUCTION

THE NATIVE PEOPLE of New Mexico and Arizona have been making pottery for about two thousand years. Their ceramics reveal a love of grace and beauty as well as skills refined over centuries. Pottery is an honored tradition, for pots have held the food and water of countless generations of *Pueblo* families and still play a role in ancient ceremonies. They provide income now as in the past, when many villages traded pots for food and other necessities as well as for treasures such as shells and turquoise.

Pottery, as perhaps no other medium, reflects the culture of its maker. Archeologists often find it their most helpful tool in classifying peoples and reconstructing past events. Each piece is different, however, even when based on old traditions, and today's potters are more innovative than ever. Just because a potter is from a certain pueblo does not mean that her work—most potters are women—will adhere to the customary style of that pueblo.

Simply stated, pottery is clay that has been formed and *fired*. But this basic definition masks a series of careful steps that begin in the earth and finish with a lyrical expression of the human spirit. For at each stage, traditional potters pray to and thank the source of their materials and their inspiration.

Preparing the clay can be the most time-consuming part of producing a pot. First, the clay must be collected. Then it must be sorted, ground, sifted, soaked, and dried, sometimes repeatedly and not necessarily in that order. In most cases, potters next add a *temper* of sand, finely crushed rock, or ground pottery *sherds* to keep the clay from shrinking and cracking when it is fired.

After many hours, the *paste* is ready. Beginning with a tortilla of clay, the potter lays it in a *puki*, a bowl-shaped support such as a basket, broken bowl, or hollow in a bed of sand, and attaches a rope of clay (a *fillet*) to its edge. Coiling more fillets on top of that one, the potter pinches them together and thins them with a scraper made of a potsherd, piece of gourd, stone, or anything handy of the right shape. To enlarge the diameter of the pot, the potter might use a longer fillet. Alternatively, especially with smaller pieces, some potters begin by making a straight-sided cylinder they then scrape and smooth into a rounded shape. After smoothing its surface, potters may attach pieces of clay in the form of ropes, animals, or ears of corn to decorate the pot. Then the potter sets the piece aside to dry, perhaps for several days. When it is *leather hard*, some carve a design into the side or rim of their pot.

Once it is completely dry, the pot is sanded to perfect its shape and remove any signs of its making—such as fingerprints. The potter may *slip* all or part of the piece to create a smooth surface and in some cases, to color it. The pot is next polished with a smooth stone, a very delicate procedure. *Sgraffito* is the technique of shallowly scraping through the slip before firing, which exposes the clay underneath.

Finally, a potter may paint a design on the pot. Many use a brush they make themselves of *yucca* fibers. Black paint may be made of ground minerals, or of boiled beeweed (called *guaco*) or tansy mustard. Various clays produce shades of red, orange, and yellow paint.

After all this, the moment of truth arrives: the pot is ready to be fired. This is a critical stage, when pots can crack or explode. Pots are supported on a rack and shielded, often with metal objects such as flattened tin cans or license plates. The fuel—usually sheep or cow dung but sometimes wood or coal—is piled under, around, and over the pottery and ignited. If oxygen is permitted to reach the piece, warm colors may develop. If the pots are smothered during the firing process, they will be black.

Not all Pueblo potters still take every step. Some just paint *greenware*, which is not considered true Pueblo pottery. Others use electric kilns to fire their pieces instead of firing them outside. At one time, buyers rejected pieces with *fire clouds* on them; now fire clouds are often sought out as proof that the pot has been fired outside and not in a kiln. In part because of the time and work involved, pottery produced in the old-fashioned way fetches higher prices.

When you are dealing with handmade objects, you will never find a "perfect" piece, but a pot should be fairly symmetrical in shape. Polished pots should be uniformly glossy and painted designs should be neat and clear. Cracks diminish the value of a pot, but some cracked pots look just as pretty on the shelf.

In many pueblos, there are families that have made fine pottery for generations. Collectors often take an interest in the work of a particularly gifted potter and her descendants.

Some potters and purchasers prefer very traditional pots, while others are more intrigued by innovative pieces. Neither is "better" than the other. Purchasers can find a wide selection of different styles at shops in Southwestern towns and cities. Alternatively, some collectors like to go directly to the homes of potters who put small signs in their windows advertising pottery for sale in the pueblos themselves. It can be fun to meet the maker of your pot and gain insights about its origins, for choosing a pot can be like making a new friend.

Italicized terms are explained in the Glossary.

FROM THE BONES OF THE SANGRE DE CRISTOS— MICACEOUS POTTERY

Four pueblos—Taos, Picurís, Nambé, and Tesuque—lie nestled into the passes and foothills of the Sangre de Cristo Mountains. The people of these pueblos make their pottery with clays containing the glittery mineral mica, obtained from the metamorphic rocks of the mountains. When fired, these clays turn bronze, orange, or golden, with shiny flecks of mica in them. Traditional micaceous pots are not painted, but fire clouds enhance their beauty with unforeseeable patterns.

"A bean pot is very useful to cook meat in there, too, in the same pot. Cook beans one time, the next time you cook beans with cabbage or anything on top of the stove, right on the burner."

Virginia Romero, Taos

TAOS

THE POTTERY of the famous northern Tiwa pueblo of Taos is deceptively simple in appearance. A thick coil of clay may be applied to the outside to form a wavy decorative border or designs may be punched into the clay walls, but generally, decoration is spare to non-existent. The pot's graceful shape is its central appeal; no complex painted designs interfere with its integrity. Its character lies in its potential use-fulness, even if the piece is intended only for display. Taos potters are especially well-known for their elegant, lidded bean pots. The pueblo's name comes from a Taos word meaning "in the village."

PICURÍS

PICURÍS IS A SMALL, northern Tiwa pueblo tucked into a lovely valley high in a pass of the Sangre de Cristos. (Their name is probably from a word in the unrelated Jémez language meaning "at the mountain gap.") Picurís shares with Taos a long tradition of micaceous pottery, although the unpainted utilitarian pots made at Picurís are somewhat thinner than those made elsewhere. A slip of mica is sometimes smoothed over a Picurís pot before it is fired, and while fire clouds may be its only decoration, potters more often apply thick ropes, beads, or little animals made of clay to their pots. The useful and often winsome shapes of Picurís pots range from small sugar bowls to large coffee pots and jars for flour and cookies.

" Pots of ours —
it's very handy
in any way.

Making pottery
too is sacred."

Virginia Duran, Picurís

Although unpainted micaceous ware had been made since 1600, it became the dominant style in the mountain pueblos after they rebelled against the Spanish three times in the late seventeenth century. The chaos of that era brought about many changes and sometimes, simplification in pottery styles. The pueblos of the mountains emulated the practical, spartan pottery shapes of their warrior neighbors, the Jicarilla Apaches, and did away with painted decoration.

Anthony Duran, Picurís, 1994

NAMBÉ

THE NAME NAMBÉ is from the Tewa words *nan*, meaning "earth" and *be?*, meaning "roundness." Although the people of Nambé are Tewa, the potters of this pueblo at the foot of the Sangre de Cristos have long made micaceous cooking pots like their Northern Tiwa neighbors. Historically, Nambé was also known for very plain, black utility ware.

Both of these pottery types dwindled along with other cultural activities in Nambé following World War II, when the population dropped to fewer than four hundred people. But during the revival of cultural identity among Native Americans during the 1970s, Nambé potters began to produce micaceous ware again. They also borrowed a range of styles from other pueblos, including both red and black polished wares as well as matte and polished *polychrome*. Painted designs include feathers, animals, pawprints, the plumed water serpent, and kachina faces, rendered in black, reddish-orange, bluish gray, and white.

" *If you've ever worked with clay, you know what clay can do. If you mix your clay the right texture, why, you can do just about anything — any form.*"

Virginia Gutierrez, Nambé

14

Virginia Gutierrez, Nambé, 1980

TESUQUE

THE TEWA PUEBLO of Tesuque (the name is from *teʼúgé*, "at a narrow place") lies just nine miles north of Santa Fe, yet is the most conservative of the Tewa pueblos.

At one time, Tesuque potters used the same clay and slip as their Tewa neighbors at San Ildefonso, to make black-on-cream and polychrome wares. As tourists began to visit the pueblo in the 1880s, a great deal of pottery was made for them. Tesuque potters mass-produced curious little "rain god" figurines as souvenirs. Some scholars see this as the beginning of a deterioration in quality there, and the quantity of ceramics declined soon thereafter. Tesuque pottery revived somewhat in the 1970s, again in response to the interest of visitors who tended to buy figurines and pottery with amusing decorations such as appliquéd animals and faces. Today, Tesuque produces mostly micaceous ware as well as burnished black pottery, the irrepressible rain gods, and some pieces that have been brightly decorated with poster paints after firing.

Unsigned, Tesuque, 1970

POJOAQUE

POJOAQUE ARTISANS once made micaceous ware. They no longer produce pottery in any distinctive style, but rather make a range of types derived from other pueblos.

" I've had a lot of backing from all my family, my people, my community. They want me to continue doing this."

Virginia Gutierrez, Nambé, married into Pojoaque

Thelma and Joe Talachy, Pojoaque, 1989

The Tewa pueblos of San Ildefonso and Santa Clara are most famous for their shiny black pottery, but both also make glossy red ware. The colors come from the way the pots are fired: allowing oxygen to reach the pot produces red; *smothering* a pot results in black.

SAN ILDEFONSO

SAN ILDEFONSO PRODUCES what is probably the most famous style of Pueblo pottery, the matte-painted, black-on-black ware developed by Maria and Julian Martinez about 1919. Potters shape their pots of tan clay, then evenly apply a red slip over the body and polish it. Finally, the design is painted on with thin, buff-colored slip, and the pot is fired in a smothering atmosphere. The design can be very elaborate—the water serpent is a common motif—and it is often borrowed from the prehistoric Mimbres culture, which favored images of animals or rows of stylized feathers. Potters also carve leather-hard pots in a technique that developed at San

" To get the clay is very hard—dig and dig—take it home, soak it and strain it. I pray before I go. I don't just go and get it and be greedy."

Blue Corn, San Ildefonso

Ildefonso and Santa Clara around 1930. They make black and reddish-orange on cream polychrome pottery as well, much like that made in earlier centuries.

Maria Martinez, San Ildefonso, courtesy of Dennis and Janis Lyon Collection

SANTA CLARA

At SANTA CLARA Pueblo, pottery making is a dynamic endeavor. With around two hundred potters—more than any other pueblo except perhaps Ácoma—there is considerable experimentation in style and method in an atmosphere of friendly competition. Production is prolific and of very high quality. While most pueblos are making smaller and smaller pots, some Santa Clara potters produce very large *ollas*. A number make polychrome pottery using black, grayish-blue, orange, and yellow paints, but most of the work here is either black or red.

Santa Clara potters have long made plain black pottery, but they developed their highly polished, often carved, black and red wares around the 1930s. Simple decorative images such as water serpents are *carved* into dry, leather-hard pots before they are fired, then sometimes matte-painted. A bear paw design, distinct to Santa Clara pottery, is sometimes pressed into the soft clay before it is slipped and polished. Sgraffito is increasingly popular as well.

" A piece of pottery is just like a little baby: watch it all the time. Just tend to it a lot."

Mary Cain, Santa Clara

Quite a few figurines are made, and the late Helen Shupla adapted an earlier shape into the elegant *melon bowl*.

Margaret Tafoya, courtesy of Gallery 10, Scottsdale

San Juan Pottery

The Tewa Pueblo of San Juan lies in a fertile spot near the confluence of the Chama River and the Rio Grande. For centuries, the potters of San Juan made polished red and black pottery very similar to that of Santa Clara, and durable tan pottery decorated with a wide band of red slip that was often purchased for practical uses by nearby Hispanic villages. In the 1930s, an increasing number of artists and visitors from Taos and Santa Fe presented a growing market. In response, several potters of the pueblo developed a distinctive style based on pieces of *incised* gray pottery dated c. 1450-1500, which they found in the ruins of Potsuwi'i, an ancestral village across the Rio Grande.

" You learn by feeling. You set it down, move away from it; turning it, using the gourds too."

Mary Archuleta, Santa Clara, married into San Juan

The "new" style is a blend of the ancient gray ware and the historic tan-with-red-middle pottery. Rims and bases of pots are now slipped and polished red and the middle is left as unslipped tan clay. Geometric designs—often made

24

up of many fine, parallel lines—are usually incised into the tan field and then painted with sparkly micaceous slip. Other designs, including water serpents, feathers, steps, spirals, and scallops, may be carved and then painted with red, buff, and white matte paints.

Rosita de Herrera, San Juan, 1975

Although there are considerable differences in the ceramic styles of the seven Keres-speaking pueblos, typically all of them are elaborately painted with black (and sometimes reddish) designs on cream slip.

COCHITÍ

COCHITÍ ARTISANS have made figurines of people and animals for centuries. These figurines were popular with visitors in the 1880s, but are now sought after even more since Helen Cordero came up with her "storytellers" in 1964. Usually painted in the traditional Cochití style of black on cream—with red filling some fields—these figurines may be of humans or animals.

Figurines sometimes find their way onto Cochití pots, which may have bears, lizards, or other creatures clinging to their rims. The rims are encircled with a fine black line that has a *line break* in it. Traditional pots are painted reddish-brown on their bases and insides. They are then coated with many layers of a cream slip that causes guaco to turn black (pueblos without this slip use a mineral paint to achieve black). Black- and/or red-painted Cochití designs represent the natural world: clouds, lightning, and rain; birds, animals, and flowers.

" *Taking pots out late in the evening they glow red in their mouths — real pretty.*"

Mary Trujillo, Cochiti

Helen Cordero, Cochiti, courtesy of Heard Museum, Phoenix

SANTO DOMINGO

BOLD, ANCIENT DESIGNS distinguish Santo Domingo pottery from other styles. These large, blocky motifs reflect the nature of this most conservative of the Keres pueblos. Santo Domingo elders frown upon the portrayal of sacred designs, human figures, and most animals on pots that are made for sale. Potters do use guaco and ochre-based red paints on cream slip to depict images of birds, flowers, corn plants, and certain stylized animals. Some assert themselves instead with thick lines and big panels of repeated shapes such as scallops, zigzags, and circles that are often symmetrical, always balanced. Encircling lines have a line break in them. Pots are made of tan clay slipped with cream, although some potters use a red slip on the base or even cover their whole pot with red.

" I would say that our pottery is a lot different from all the other pueblos even though it's called polychrome. Each pueblo has their own paints and styles."

Robert Tenorio, Santo Domingo

Santo Domingo has a history of vigorous trading over long distances. The shapes of the pueblo's pottery remain sturdy and functional, as the use of traditional pottery is still woven into the ceremonial and day-to-day life of the pueblo.

Robert Tenorio, Santo Domingo, 1982

SANTA ANA

ALTHOUGH THEY NOW live in more modern villages, the potters of Santa Ana return to their old pueblo on the north bank of the Jémez River to collect red clay, which they temper with sand from the river. They slip their pots with white or buff, and paint them with simple old designs, mostly geometrics or abstract images of clouds, flowers, and sometimes *turkey eyes*. Santa Ana potters use a lot of red paint in decorating their pots, with or without the black outline customary at other pueblos. They paint the bases of their pots red as well as the insides of the rims, which they encircle with a thin band that often has a line break. They paint thick lines and strong shapes on the bulging part of the pot between the two.

" *Some look for perfection. Made by hand—very rarely you come across a perfect one. All individual, just like we are.*"

Gladys Paquin, Laguna, raised at Santa Ana

The Santa Ana tradition all but died out until Eudora Montoya began teaching others in the pueblo how to make pots in the 1970s. Today, only a few potters make these unique ollas.

M. Montoya, Santa Ana, 1994

31

ZIA

THE LITTLE JÉMEZ River pueblo of Zia has an ancient, unbroken tradition of exquisite pottery. The land surrounding the pueblo is poor for farming, and so the people of Zia long traded their ceramics for food, often with Jémez and also with San Felipe (which as a result, never developed fine pottery). Zia artisans still continue with their pleasing old style, which has been so highly regarded for centuries.

Zia potters use the same red clay as the people at Santa Ana do, but they are the only Pueblo potters to temper their clay with crushed black basalt. Their black paint is made from iron-rich concretions that weather out of the local sandstone. They slip most pots with white or buff although red is sometimes used, and paint the bases of their pots red with solid double lines above to set off the area they will fill with lively black and red designs. Zia motifs are naturalistic, with twining florals and arabesques. Often, thick curved arches or "rainbow bands" enclose their hallmark, the Zia bird, or a deer or flowering plant.

" *Most of the older pots have things hidden in the design, shapes hidden in spaces between the colors ... They were trying to make things hard for the archaeologists!*"

Marcellus Medina, Zia

Elizabeth Medina, Zia, 1992

ÁCOMA

ÁCOMA HAS ALWAYS enjoyed a lively trade in its pottery, and today supports a vigorous ceramics industry. Hundreds of artisans produce thousands of pots for shops across the Southwest as well as for visitors to their ancestral village, which crowns a high mesa sixty-five miles west of Albuquerque. To hasten the process, a number of Ácoma potters now just paint greenware rather than collect, process, and shape their own clay. Ácoma ceramics come in a wide array of shapes from ollas to animals to ashtrays.

Pots made at Ácoma tend to be very strong, yet have thin walls. The white clay is tempered with crushed potsherds. Some pots are partly or entirely *corrugated*. Potters use black hematite mixed with beeweed juice to paint elaborate designs on a white background of *kaolin* slip, often above an orange-painted base. It is not unusual for a painted design to completely cover an Ácoma pot. Since the 1940s, fastidious geometric arrangements of fine lines derived from ancient potsherds have

" *There's yucca out there. There's bee-plant out there. Everything's there.*"

Dolores Lewis Garcia, Ácoma

become a favorite style, sometimes with sections colored in with orange. However, Ácoma potters still paint flowers and animals also—including some abstract creatures inspired by the Mimbres culture—as well as *split rectangles*.

Dorothy Torivio, Ácoma, courtesy of Gallery 10, Scottsdale

LAGUNA

LAGUNA WAS FOUNDED by refugees from the Spanish reconquest of the Rio Grande Valley in the late seventeenth century. Laguna pottery almost died out in the twentieth century, but beginning in 1973, a federally funded program led by local potter Evelyn Cheromiah revived the craft here. The potters of Laguna use basically the same materials to make a ware that is similar in many ways to that of its close Keres neighbor, Ácoma. However, Laguna's painted designs tend to be simpler, somewhat bolder, and less delicate. More of the pale background is left open in most cases, although sometimes even experts have a difficult time distinguishing between pottery of the two pueblos.

Evelyn Cheromiah, Laguna, 1987

ISLETA

IN THE LATE nineteenth century, people from Laguna moved to Isleta Pueblo, a southern Tiwa pueblo on the Rio Grande fifteen miles south of Albuquerque. The local potters had made a plain red ware before Laguna introduced polychrome. Today, the potters of Isleta generally make a polychrome based on the Laguna style, but modified by the addition of white to the paints, which turns them into soft pastels.

The southern Tiwa of Sandía, fifteen miles north of Albuquerque, make no pottery now.

" Every one of our potteries has their own personality—just like every day is different—even when you try to make the same design again."

Gladys Paquin, Laguna

Stella Teller, Isleta, 1980

REDISCOVERING THE CLAY—
JÉMEZ POTTERY

THERE IS GREAT VARIETY in modern Jémez pottery, but in general its colors are subtle: buff, cream, black, and russet on buff- or red-slipped tan clay. Potters make bowls and jars, double-spouted wedding vases, and figurines such as owls, storytellers, and people in scenes of daily life. Sgraffito is a popular technique, and decorative motifs include geometrics, corn, feathers, clouds, and the sun.

Jémez is the last pueblo to speak Towa (*Jémez* is a Spanish spelling of the Towa word for "us"). Jémez fiercely resisted the Spanish reconquest in the late seventeenth century and stopped producing their black-on-white pottery during those turbulent years. They have good farmland, so they traded crops for pots with neighboring Zia. Their own traditions forgotten, Jémez potters have adapted the styles of other pueblos in reviving their ceramics industry over the past fifty years. At first, they made inexpensive pots decorated with poster paint but now use mostly mineral-based

" We're not making a name for ourselves; we are making a name for Jémez."

Maxine Toya, Jémez

paints, sometimes mixed with guaco. In the 1970s, Jémez potters Evelyn Vigil and Juanita Toledo participated in the rediscovery of lead-based glaze paints for a program at the abandoned Towa Pueblo of Pecos, which is now managed by the National Park Service.

J. Pecos, Jémez, courtesy of Heard Museum, Phoenix

IMAGES FROM THE PAST—
ZUNI POTTERY

ZUNI POTTERY BEARS beautiful, ancient designs. With black or brown and red paint on white or red slip, potters skillfully depict rainbirds, flowers, feathers, rosettes, scrollwork, cross-hatching, and deer with *heartlines*. Pots may have a brown base and usually have black or red rims. Encircling lines have breaks in the old-fashioned way. These designs are so time-consuming that pots are usually fired in electric kilns to avoid smoke clouds and other potential problems of outdoor firing. The clay is tempered with crushed potsherds.

"This year we are going to have to do eleven big bowls and give them away to the mudheads. They only use them on special occasions."

Randy Nahohai, Zuni

Zuni is New Mexico's most populated pueblo; its language is unique (although perhaps related to California native languages). Until fairly recently, few pots were made at Zuni apart from ceremonial pieces. Young Zunis could learn ceramics at the high school, however, and finally two non-Zuni teachers, Daisy Hooee Nampeyo (Hopi-Tewa) and Jenny Laate (Ácoma)—together with Zuni potter Josephine Nahohai—brought about a pottery renaissance in the 1970s. They examined old Zuni pots in museum collections and revived the traditional designs.

Courtesy of Heard Museum, Phoenix

WARMTH OF THE EARTH—
HOPI POTTERY

THE GLOWING CHARACTER of Hopi pottery comes from the clay itself. Potters use gray clay that turns various shades of apricot when fired, and yellow clay that turns red. Mineral variations in the gray clay create uneven but lovely golden patterns when fired. Pots may be unslipped or slipped with the same clays. Minerals mixed with guaco are used for black paint; yellow clay slip for red. Hopi pots tend to be squat—seed jars, open bowls, and ollas are often much wider than they are high—but there are also cylindrical vases.

Hopi people live on and around three mesas in Arizona. Some white ware with appliquéd decorations is made in Third Mesa villages, but most pottery is made at First Mesa, where descendants of Tewa refugees have lived for three centuries in "Tewa Village," or Hano. (Hopi is an Uto-Aztecan language not related to Tewa). In the 1880s, the Tewa Village potter Nampeyo and

" . . . And then when you are doing your work like this you should have a smiling face and happy with your children, your family."

Daisy Hooee, Hopi-Tewa

her Hopi husband, Lesou, began to recreate the pottery of Sikyatki, a ruined Hopi village below First Mesa. The abstract, asymmetrical motifs of most Hopi pottery stem from this Sikyatki style, and include feathers, birds, and rain images, often with stippled or finely lined sections.

Nampeyo, Hopi

GLOSSARY

Carved: decoration cut deeply into a pot.

Corrugated: pottery with rows of little indentations on its surface.

Fillet: rope of clay that is coiled on a base to create the walls of a pot.

Fire cloud: dark smudge on a pot that was fired outdoors, caused by a piece of burning fuel touching the pot.

Fired: baked at a high temperature.

Greenware: unfired clay objects, mass-produced in molds.

Guaco: a paint made by boiling beeweed.

Heartline: painted arrow leading from the mouth into the chest of an animal motif.

Incised: fine lines scratched through the surface of an unfired pot.

Kaolin: a very fine, soft white clay.

Leather hard: stage of dryness at which an unfired pot is no longer malleable.

Line break: gap left in an encircling line.

Melon bowl: rounded bowl with thick, vertical ribs.

Mudheads: ceremonial clowns.

Ollas: Spanish for "pots."

Oxidizing atmosphere: the condition in which air is allowed to reach the pot throughout the firing process.

Paste: mixture of clay and temper.

Polychrome: painted with various colors.

Pueblo: Spanish for "people" or "town." Now, the traditional people of the Rio Grande and Jémez River valleys as well as Laguna, Ácoma, Zuni, and Hopi.

Puki: bowl-shaped object used to support the curved bottom of a pot.

Reducing atmosphere: occurs when oxygen is kept from pottery during firing.

Sgraffito: decoration scraped very shallowly into a pot's surface.

Sherd: piece of broken pottery; sometimes spelled shard to reflect the British pronunciation.

Slip: liquid clay applied over a pot to smooth and/or color it. Some slips have an important chemical reaction with certain paints.

Smothering: covering the pots with powdered fuel—usually manure—during firing.

Split rectangles: design element in which a rectangle is divided in half diagonally and each half is decorated differently.

Temper: gritty material added to clay to prevent a piece from shrinking or breaking as it dries or is fired.

Turkey eyes: design element consisting of a dot encircled by white space bordered by a dark color.

Yucca: very fibrous evergreen plant that grows throughout the Southwest, used by some potters as a paintbrush.